MUSIC MINUS ONE

DVOŘÁK

Antonín Dvořák
Piano Trio, Op. 90
"Dumky"

MMO CD 3037

COMPACT DISC PAGE AND BAND INFORMATION

Music Minus One

MMO CD 3037
MMO Cass. 63

Dvořák
"Dumky" Piano Trio in Em, Opus 90

PRINTED IN CANADA

Antonin Dvořák

Piano Trio, Op. 90

"Dumky"

4 taps (1 measure) precede music.

Allegro quasi doppio movimento.

Allegro quasi doppio movimento.

cresc.
f
ff
ffz
ff
ff
f
Ped.
fz
ff
fz fz fz fz
fz fz fz fz
sul G
ff
poco ritard.
ff
poco ritard.
ff
ff
ritard.

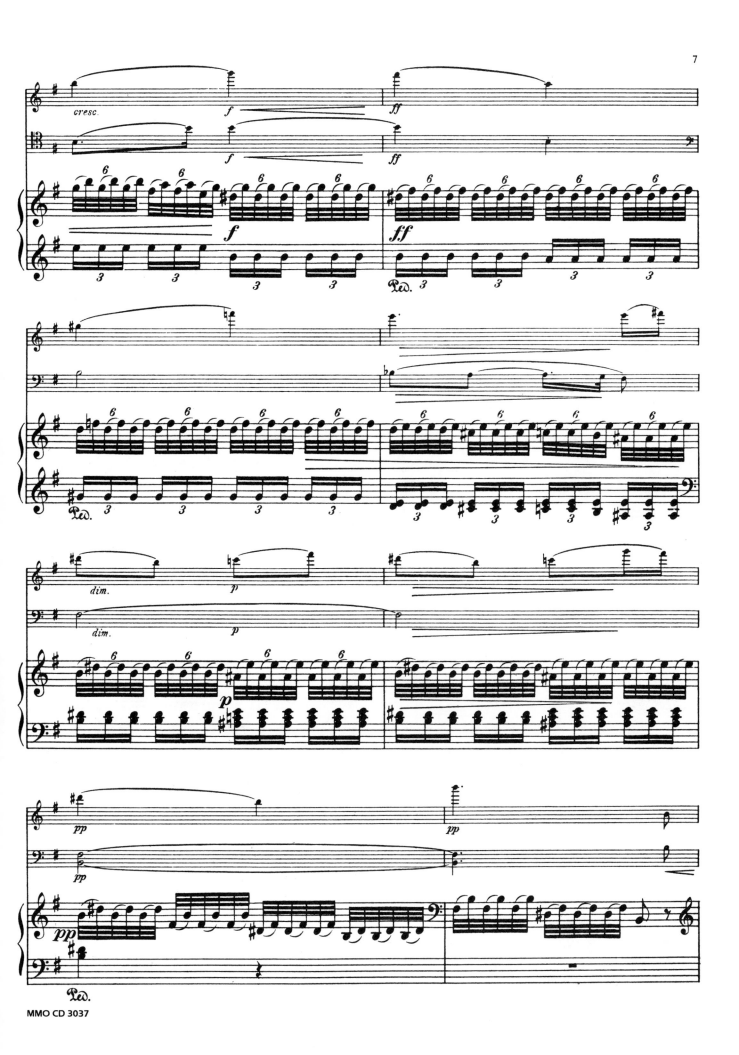

8

Poco adagio.

4 taps (1 measure) precede music.

con sord.

Poco adagio.

Vivace.
senza sord.
pp
pp
Vivace.
marcato il Basso
fz poco a poco
fp cresc.
fz
fp poco a poco
fp cresc.
poco a poco
cresc.
fz
marcato
fz

18

3 taps (1 measure) precede music

20

28

32

Lento maestoso.

4 taps (1 measure) precede music. **Lento maestoso.**

Poco più mosso.

Poco più mosso.

Più mosso.

Più mosso.

40

MUSIC MINUS ONE

Antonín Dvořák
Piano Trio, Op. 90
"Dumky"

MMO CD 3037

MMO CD 3037   **MUSIC MINUS ONE** *50 Executive Boulevard • Elmsford New York 10523-1325*